Music Manuscripts

ARTHUR SEARLE

The British Library

Published by
The British Library
Great Russell Street
London
WC1B 3DG

and 27 South Main Street
Wolfeboro, New Hampshire 03894–2069

British Library Cataloguing in Publication Data

Searle, Arthur
  Music manuscripts.
  1. Music—Manuscripts—History
  1 Title   II. British Library
  780   ML93

  ISBN 0–7123–0129–1

Library of Congress Cataloging in Publication Data

Searle, Arthur.
  Music manuscripts / Arthur Searle.
  80p.
  ISBN 0–7123–0129–1 (pbk.) : $10.95
  1. Music—History and criticism.   2. Music—
  Manuscripts—Facsimiles.   3. British Library.
  I. Title.
  ML160.S405 1987
  780'.94—dc19

Designed by Roger Davies
Typeset in Monophoto Ehrhardt
by August Filmsetting, Haydock, St Helens

Colour origination by York House Graphics, Hanwell
Printed in England by
Jolly and Barber Ltd, Rugby

FRONT COVER *see* **7; 30; 62.**

BACK COVER *see* **1.**

Acknowledgements

The author would like to thank Mr. O. W.
Neighbour in particular among his colleagues
for his help and advice.
   The British Library is grateful for
permission to reproduce particular items:
Boosey and Hawkes Music Publishers Ltd. (**66,
67, 71, 72**); Trustees of the Britten Estate (**77**);
Chester Music (**66**); The Holst Foundation (**69,
70**); Oxford University Press and Gerald
Duckworth and Co., Ltd. (**73**); Peters Edition
Ltd., London (**63**); Royal Philharmonic Society
(**50**); R.V.W. Ltd., (**68, 76**); Universal Edition,
Vienna (Alfred A. Kalms Ltd) (**64, 65**).

1 *This page and opposite* Canon in
honour of King Henry VIII
A double canon for two bassus and two
contratenor voices, to a Latin text
celebrating the union of the houses of
York and Lancaster. The two parts
appear on facing pages in the original
manuscript.
Royal MS 11.E.XI, ff.2v,3. 487 × 680 mm.
(whole opening)

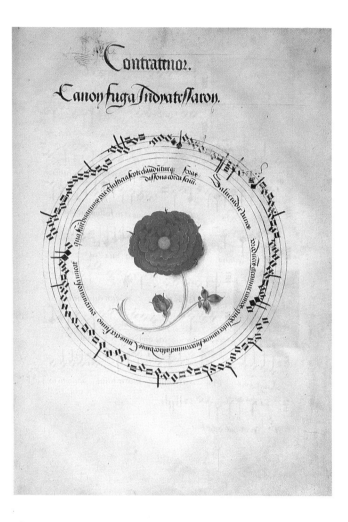

Contents

orat. Omnes ergo exultemus tante potesta
ti. Offerentes regis vasa sue maiestati.

Tunc princi
pes dicant. Ecce sunt ante fa   ciem
        Interim apparebit dextra in conspectu
tuam. regis scribens in pariete. Mane. The
chel. Phares. Quam mox rex stupefactus clamabit.
Vocate mathe

maticos caldeos et ariolos. Auruspices inqui
rite et magos introducite. Tunc adducent magi
rite et magos introducite. qui dicent Regi

Rex in eternum vive. Adsumus ecce tibi.

O si scripturam hanc legerit et sensum ape
ruerit: Sub illius potentia subdetur baby

Introduction

The appearance of a music manuscript will always reflect the circumstances and purpose of its creation as well as the nature of the music it contains. The agitation of the satraps at Belshazzar's feast as the hand appears writing upon the wall is visible in the complex melismas of the music they sing in the *Play of Daniel*, written by the choristers of Beauvais cathedral in the thirteenth century (**2**). Three hundred years later, at the court of King Henry VIII of England, the four-part canon 'Salve radix' has a more artfully contrived visual message, with the music curling round the exquisitely drawn Tudor rose of the new dynasty (**1**). Another three hundred years on, and Puccini's hasty scribble of some of his first ideas for the suicide scene at the end of *Madam Butterfly* is entirely without artistic appeal, yet conveys to the eye all of the drama that emerges in the finished opera (**60**).

The British Library's collection of music manuscripts

The printed and manuscript music in the British Library together forms a collection which is among the foremost in the world. The purpose of this book is to reproduce a representative selection from the music manuscripts and to relate the chosen examples to at least some of the developments in musical history from the middle ages to our own day. Much has to be left out simply because of the size of the book. Composers can for the most part be represented by only one item; the Handel manuscripts are virtually a complete musical archive, and the Library's Elgar collection is the largest anywhere, but only *Messiah* (**30**) and the *Enigma* Variations (**62**) can be shown. While these are probably their best-known works, on their own they inevitably present a limited view of each composer.

The pattern of the book reflects the collections themselves. After showing a very few of the Library's most outstanding medieval music manuscripts, the first main section concentrates on English sources for the sixteenth and seventeenth centuries. This is followed by a selection of important eighteenth- and nineteenth-century German and Viennese composers, examples of later nineteenth-century works, and finally the leading figures of the British twentieth-century revival, set in context with examples of some of the most important of their European contemporaries. This is the profile of the body of music manuscripts built up from the foundation of the British Museum in 1753 and still being added to by the British Library. From time to time existing large collections have been added to the holdings, often as the result of a gift to the nation. Among the most important musically are the old Royal Library, presented by George III in 1757 (and of which the choir-book containing the 'Salve radix' canon is part), the Royal Music Library (which includes the Handel autographs), presented by Queen Elizabeth II in 1957, and the Stefan Zweig Collection, given to the Library in 1986.

George III's fondness for the music of Handel and Stefan Zweig's admiration for Mozart are reflected in their collections, and the Library's own cumulative collection has benefited from the tastes of individuals at many points. The J. S. Bach manuscript (**28**) was treasured by the early

2 'The Play of Daniel'
An early thirteenth-century music drama used as part of the celebration of Christmas at Beauvais Cathedral. The stupefied amazement of King Belshazzar as the hand appears writing on the wall is indicated in the rubric: 'rex stupefactus clamabit' (in red, like all the 'stage directions').
Egerton MS 2615, f.97. 220 × 140 mm.

5

nineteenth-century Bach enthusiasts in England and eventually bequeathed to the Museum by Samuel Wesley's daughter Eliza. The sonatas by Domenico Scarlatti (31) were preserved as a result of similar enthusiasm at a time when the music was little known, and the Schubert piano sonata was a gift from the pianist F. E. Perabo. The presence of important English Renaissance sources, such as the Baldwin (16), Cosyn and Forster books, in the Royal Music Library, stems directly from the archaeological interest in the music of that period fostered by Burney and Hawkins in the late eighteenth century. The interest created by their work also ensured the availability of similar manuscripts for purchase by the Museum in the nineteenth century. Factors of this kind have always created opportunities for adding to the collections. The acquisition by the Museum of a number of Beethoven sketchbooks (among them 37) in the 1880s is an outstanding example of the benefits to be gained.

The expanding collection of manuscripts of twentieth-century British composers arises from a rather different set of circumstances. In the years since the Second World War it has increasingly become possible to acquire substantial collections either directly from the composers themselves, or from their families and heirs. This process was set underway by a series of generous gifts, and the manuscripts acquired over the last forty years or so now form a source for research comparable to the sixteenth- and seventeenth-century music manuscripts in the Library. Examples from three of those gifts are shown here: Elgar (62), Vaughan Williams (68, 76) and Holst (69). They must represent all the other composers of those generations (among them Ethel Smyth, Rutland Boughton, Bax, and Ireland), just as Britten (77) and Tippett (78) are only the most important examples of later acquisitions.

In collections of manuscripts such as those of Vaughan Williams or Tippett now in the Library it is possible to trace the growth of a single work though various stages of its composition, as well as the more general development of the composer's methods and achievements. Only a very few autograph manuscripts survive from before the 1630s, so that the earlier sources provide quite different information, concerned with what music was played, the way it was performed, and often how the actual musical text changed when it was written down in different places or by different generations. The features of the choir-book from the court of Henry VIII with which the first main section begins (7) are to be found in almost all of the manuscripts of the sixteenth and early seventeenth centuries: separate pieces by different composers are brought together in a single volume, their selection governed by the purpose for which the whole group was intended. Categories such as vocal music (sacred or secular), instrumental works, or keyboard pieces, can define the scope of an anthology of this sort, depending on who compiled it and where – for example, at court or in one of the great ecclesiastical foundations. The categories could change or become mixed if the purpose or ownership of the volume changed, for music manuscripts were useful objects, to be kept and added to. Equally, in some instances different kinds of music were present from the start, at the whim of an amateur simply copying into his musical 'commonplace book' pieces which caught his fancy.

An important and increasingly explored part of musical history is preserved in volumes like these. Comparison between such manuscripts, and, indeed, the growing amount of printed music being issued during the period (much of it in 'anthology' format), makes it possible to trace the development of musical repertories, and, where pieces appear in more than one source, the transmission and authenticity of musical texts.

The earliest autograph manuscripts in this book have something of the nature of the sixteenth-century sources: the pieces by Henry Lawes, Locke and Purcell (23, 22, 25) all come from anthologies, but these anthologies are the composers' fair copy books of their own works. Like these, the later autographs chosen for inclusion have the impact of the composer's own marks on paper; they give quite literally the composer's own view of his music. In addition they represent a specific stage in the composition of the work in question. They vary widely in appearance, encompassing hasty sketches by Beethoven (37), Puccini (60) and Vaughan Williams (68), a composition draft in short score by Britten (77), and fair copies of their newest works which Webern in 1909 (64) and Berg in 1934 (65) wrote out for their teacher Schoenberg. Bach's fugue in A flat from book two of *Das Wohltemperirte Clavier* (28) comes from a manuscript written out for performers to use. Handel worked on *Messiah* in the knowledge that his copyists would prepare the score and parts for performance, so that minor alterations at least could be made once their work was done. Because Mozart himself saw his six 'Haydn' string quartets through the press, the autographs by no means represent his final thoughts on the pieces, and there are in fact quite significant differences between them and the authoritative first edition (35, 24). When looking at manuscripts of this kind there is just as much need to consider the circumstances under which they were written as there is in the more obvious case of the medieval and Renaissance sources which precede them here.

Medieval Music

The *Play of Daniel* adapts the western ecclesiastical tradition of plainchant to dramatic purposes, and uses notation giving pitch but not length or rhythm. The late thirteenth-century Trouvères song (4) is also written in non-mensural notation, and is shaped in part by its secular verse; like the Troubadours in Provence, the Trouvères in northern French speaking areas set carefully structured verses. There is a vernacular text, too, for the famous English *rota*, or round, 'Sumer is icumen in', dating from the middle of the thirteenth century (3). (It has been suggested that the alternative Latin text was added to lend respectability – the piece appears in a monastic volume.) This is a complex piece of polyphony: the main text is designed to be sung in canon by four voices, and below it is a 'pes', a kind of *cantus firmus*, for two further voices. This is the earliest surviving polyphony, and no other music for as many as six voices is known before the

Svmer is icumen in · Lhude sing cuccu · Groweþ sed and bloweþ
Perspice xpicola · que dignacio · celicus agrico —

med and springþ þe wde nu · Sing cuccu Awe bleteþ after
la · pro uitis · uicio · filio — non parcens exposu

lomb · lhouþ after calue cu · Bulluc sterteþ · bucke uerteþ
it · mortis · exicio — Qui captiuos semiuiuos

murie sing cuccu · Cuccu cuccu Wel singes þu cuccu ne swik
a supplicio — Vite donat et secum coronat in ce

Hanc rotam cantare possunt quatuor socii a paucio
ribus autem quam a tribus ut saltem duobus non debet
dici preter eos qui dicunt pedem. Canitur autem sic Tacen
tibus ceteris unus inchoat cum hijs q tenent pede Et cum uenerit
ad primam notam post crucem inchoat alius · et sic de ceteris

þu nauer nu · li so liuo ·

singli u repausent ad pausaciones scriptas
talibz spacio unius longe note ......
hoc repetit un' quocienis op' est
ing cuccu nu · Sing cuccu · faciens pausacionem in fine

ing cuccu · Sing cuccu nu
hoc dicit alius pausans in medio et non in
fine Sed immediate repetes principiu

4 Trouvère song 'La douche vois del rosignuel sauvage'
The words for this song, like the manuscript, date from the late thirteenth century, though an earlier melody is used. An annotation added in the margin identifies the poet as 'Messire Reignaut, Castellain de Couchy'.
Egerton MS 274, ff.108v, 109. 148 × 109 mm.

3 'Sumer is icumen in'
The famous *rota*, or round, dating from the middle of the thirteenth century, the earliest known English polyphony. The cross in the first line marks the point at which the four voices in turn enter, and the *pes* for two further voices is at the foot of the page. Directions, in Latin, for performance are also given.
Harley MS 978, f.11v. 190 × 125 mm.

late fifteenth century. The fourteenth-century duet *ballata* by Niccolò da Perugia (5) illustrates the Italian *ars nova*, music with increased melodic and rhythmic possibilities which followed the development of new forms of notation. Accomplished pieces like this are typical of the urban culture of Tuscany and Lombardy in this period.

These manuscripts are little more than random examples, but they give some idea of the variety and sophistication of European music before the Renaissance. The *Play of Daniel* and 'Sumer is icumen in' are unique sources; without them we should have no knowledge of these particular dramatic, melodic and polyphonic riches of thirteenth-century music. They show the kinds of material with which editors have to work to enable the music to be re-created in performance today. There is also other manuscript evidence for the importance of music in medieval life: practical music-making is illustrated in manuscripts of all kinds. Countless musical figures appear in illuminated initial letters, or decorating the margins of a page. They range from groups engaged in the solemn or joyful

5 A fourteenth-century Italian *ballata*
A two-part *ballata* 'Io vegio in grave dolo' by Niccolò da Perugia, from a manuscript including works composed from about 1340 onwards, though written at the end of the century. Niccolò was active in Florence in the second half of the fourteenth century. Francesco Landini is among the other composers represented in the volume.
Add. MS 29987, f.40.

6 The 'Old Hall' manuscript, c. 1410–15: 'Gloria' by 'Roy Henry'
This piece is written out in parts, choir-book fashion. Its composer has been identified as Henry IV, or perhaps the young Henry V before he ascended the throne.

in terra pax ho[m]inibus bo ne volun ta tis. Lau

da mus te. bene di ci mus te. adoramus te. glorificamus te. gracias

agimus ti bi propter magnam gloriam tuam. Domine de us rex ce

les tis deus pa ter omnipotens domine fi li uni geni te ihu xp[ist]e. Domi

ne deus agnus de i filius pa tris. Qui tollis peccata mundi

misere re no bis. Qui tollis peccata mundi suscipe deprecacionem

no stram. Qui sedes ad dexteram pa tris miserere no bis.

Quoniam tu so lus sanc tus. Tu solus do mi nus. Tu so lus al tissimus

Ihesu cri ste cum sancto spiritu in glori a de i pa tris. A[men]

glorification of God, to more popular music, often represented by grotesques or animal figures. The musical scholar can make use of these too, for they provide information about the forces used in performance and the types and construction of musical instruments.

One music manuscript is outstanding among the Library's late-medieval sources. It is a choir-book of *c*. 1410–15 containing a collection of polyphonic pieces by named composers, and it is by far the earliest example to survive in England. The origins of the 'Old Hall' manuscript (**6**) are obscure – it takes its name from the Hertfordshire school which owned it previously – but it is a precious record of English liturgical music in the late fourteenth and early fifteenth century, and its importance is enhanced by its handsome appearance. The pieces in it are grouped according to their place in the liturgy; the *Gloria* by 'Roy Henry' occurs with other settings of that text, while a *Sanctus* attributed to the same composer is separated from it, in its own appropriate section. Some of the pieces are written out in score, but most are in proper choir-book format, like the *Gloria*, with the parts entered separately on each opening of the book.

The drawings of musicians reproduced in this section are taken from Arundel MS 83, Stowe MS 17 and Add. MS 49622.

7 *opposite* Josquin Desprez (*c*. 1440–1521): motet 'Missus est Gabriel angelus'
From a choir-book containing works by various European composers and designed for presentation to Henry VIII and his first queen, Katherine of Aragon. The book may have been prepared in the circle of the great Flemish court scribe Pierre Alamire, and is the work of a number of different writers: the elaborate initial letters, the music and the text underlay each inserted at different stages.
Royal MS 8.G.VII, ff.23v,24. 367 × 490 mm.

The 16th and 17th Centuries

Two powerful external influences on musical life become apparent in any collection of manuscripts from this period: religion and the monarchy. The choir-book from the court of Henry VIII (7) demonstrates the sophistication (and internationalism) to be found in the music of the royal household at the beginning of the century, and a majority of the composers in the later examples were at one time or another in the service of the Chapel Royal. There is also evidence of Henry VIII's own musical prowess (8, 9). Among the most spectacular pieces of English court music must be the forty-part motet 'Spem in alium' (17) by Thomas Tallis, who served successive monarchs from Henry to Elizabeth. The Latin text relates to the biblical story of Judith, and the motet may have formed part of the celebrations of Queen Elizabeth's fortieth birthday in 1573.

The turbulent religious history of England often intrudes into the music. Taverner's 'Westerne Wynde' mass (10) dates from late in Henry's reign, following the break with Rome, and the anthem praying for his sickly son, Edward VI, comes from a set of manuscript part-books which contain some of the very earliest Anglican church music. These influences could be felt in quite personal ways. William Byrd was a Roman Catholic, but nonetheless managed to stay enough on the right side of the law to be employed in the service of Elizabeth I (13, 14, 16). The Tregian family,

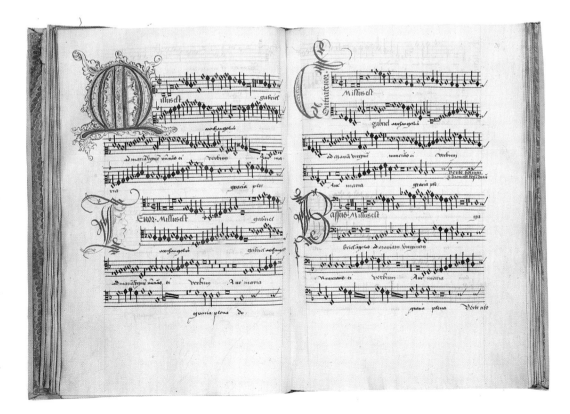

Cornish landed gentry, also adhered to the old church, and underwent exile for their beliefs. In the early years of the seventeenth century Francis Tregian compiled extraordinary manuscript assemblies of vocal and keyboard music which are now in Cambridge (the Fitzwilliam Virginal Book), London (20) and New York. He copied music from a wide variety of sources and from many countries, apparently simply as a musical exercise for his own use at home.

Most of John Dowland's pieces were intended for domestic music making, circulating widely in printed collections and in manuscript lute books. Despite this popularity, he too aspired to a court appointment; since his hopes in England in this respect were frustrated until the reign of James I, he spent time in the courts of northern Europe in the 1590s (20). One form of chamber music peculiar to England, the *In Nomine*, neatly demonstrates the possibilities of influence from one musical sphere to another. It derives from the 'in nomine' section of Taverner's mass 'Gloria tibi trinitas', which circulated widely (without its text) as instrumental music and gave rise to a whole group of complex instrumental pieces, all based on the plainchant melody of a Sarum rite antiphon. Seven *In Nomines* by Byrd have survived, in four and five parts. The piece by Robert Parsons shown here (15) is one of two he wrote in seven parts, displaying great contrapuntal ingenuity. Secular vocal part music is represented by Gibbons's 'Cries of London' (18). The 'Willow Song' (19) comes from a manuscript collection, presumably compiled for domestic use, which contains both sacred and secular pieces, among them other songs associated with the theatre.

These manuscripts show a number of different formats. Both the Josquin motet (7) and Henry VIII's 'Pastyme with good Companye' are laid out as choir-books (like the *Gloria* (6) from the Old Hall manuscript), with the parts separately entered on each opening of the volume. Most of the other vocal consort music is written out in part-books, the more usual form at this period (10, 12, 18). The Parsons *In Nomine* comes from a manuscript laid out as a table-book; the opening contains the complete piece, and the parts are written facing outwards, so that the players can perform sitting or standing around a table on which the volume lies open.

This would appear to be a unique manuscript survival in England, though Dowland, for example, used the format in publishing some of his lute songs. The Dowland piece here (20), and the 'Willow Song' both use lute tablature, where each line represents a 'course' (a number of strings, usually two, tuned in unison) on the lute. A similar system is still used for guitar accompaniments in popular music. The Tallis manuscript (17) is a striking example of a complex piece written out in score, though not in a way which might be expected. Instead of being grouped in the eight five-voice choirs that make up the work, the vocal lines are arranged eight at a time, by registers, with a 'thorough bass' line holding it all together across the centre of the page. Francis Tregian's neat scoring of the Monteverdi piece (21) was presumably made from separate published or manuscript parts.

8 Henry VIII, with his jester Will Somers.
Royal MS 2 A. XVI, f.63v.

9 Henry VIII (1491–1547); 'Pastyme with good companye'
The king was fond of music from his youth; he sang, and played the organ, lute and virginals. The 'Henry VIII Manuscript' contains a number of pieces ascribed to him, with others by such English composers as William Cornysh, Master of the Children of the Chapel Royal.
Add. MS 31922, f.14v. 305 × 210 mm.

Pastyme wt good cpanye I love & shall vntyll I dye

gruche who lust but none denye so god be plesyd ye leve wytt

I for my pastace shut syng & daunce my hart is sett all

goodly sport for my cofort who shatt me let

Pastyme wt good cpanye I love & shall tyl I dye

grruche who lust but none denye so god be plesyd ye leve

wytt I for my pastance but syng & daunce my hart is

10 John Taverner (*c.* 1490–1545): 'Western Wynde' Mass
The triplex (treble) part from the 'Gyffard Part-books', probably copied in the 1550s. The mass takes the form of a carefully planned set of 36 variations on the tune of the popular song 'Westron wynde when wyll thow blow'. The book also contains masses by Tye and Sheppard based on the same tune.
Add. MS 17803, ff.23v, 24. 204 × 254 mm.

11 'The Mulliner Book': John Redford (died 1547), 'Miserere' for organ
Redford was the most important composer of organ music in the reign of Henry VIII – the 'meane' in this piece is the centre part, shared between the two hands as indicated. Redford was one of the musicians at St Paul's cathedral where, later in the reign, Thomas Mulliner, the compiler of this anthology, was organist and choir master.
Add. MS 30513, f.58. 150 × 195 mm.

12 A prayer for Edward VI
The treble, from a set of part-books, of an anthem in the form of a prayer: 'O lorde christe Jhesu . . . we sinners do most humbly beseche thy hy maiestie to graunt thy noble servant our soveraigne lorde kyng Edward . . . that he may have thorou the ovyr all his enemys most ryall vyctory . . .'.
Royal MS, Appendix 74, f.22v. 190 × 275 mm.

11

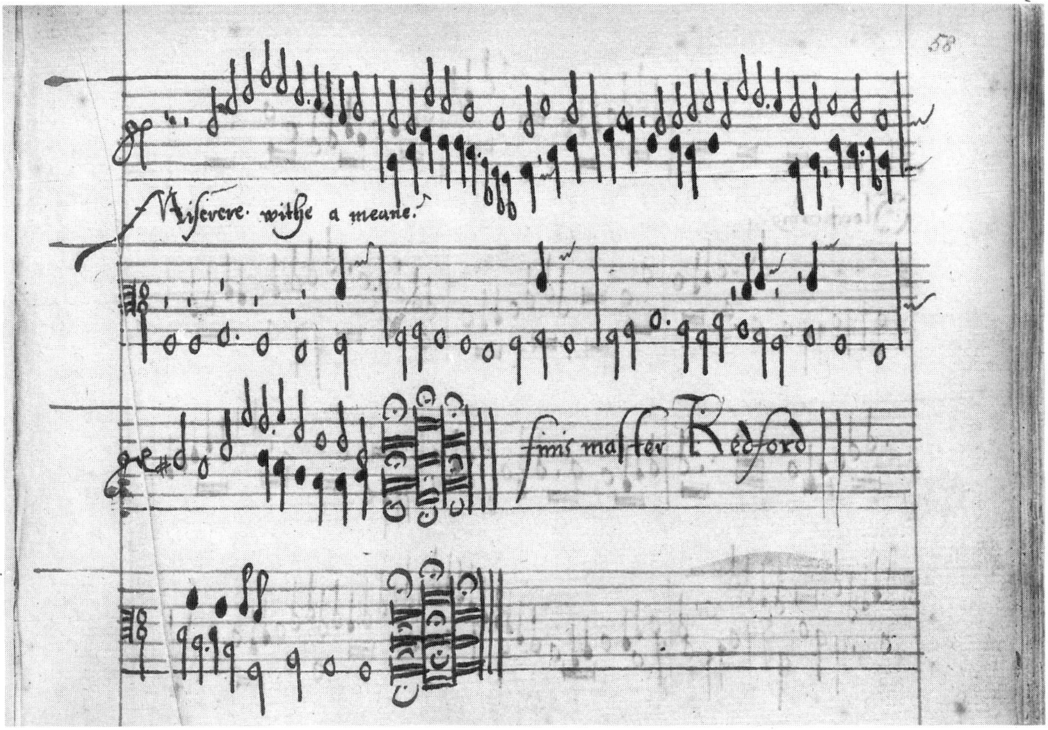
Miserere withe a meane.
finis master Redford

12

O lorde christe thu that art kyng in glory, O lorde chryste thu that art
kyng in glory, that art kyng in glory. And very perfit rote of all felicite
we sinners do most humbly beseche thy hye maiestie to graunt thy noble servant
sovereigne lorde kyng edward kyng edward, sovereigne lord kyng edward, that he may
have thorow thy ayde all his enemys most ryall vyctory most ryall vyctory, yet
further more: to the o lord we do bothe cry & call, we do bothe cry an call

13 Anthology of keyboard music compiled by Thomas Weelkes (1576–1623): William Byrd, the Quadran Pavan

The identification of the compiler of this volume, with its distinctive musical hand, as Weelkes makes it of special interest as the collection of keyboard pieces of a man whose own compositions were mostly for voices. It was possibly written about 1600.

Add. MS 30485, f.8. 293 × 192 mm.

14 William Byrd's signature from a letter in support of the impoverished wife and family of a recusant, 1581.

Egerton MS 3722.

15 Robert Parsons (*c.* 1530–1570): *In Nomine* in seven parts
An opening from a table-book which its compiler described as 'a booke of In nomines & other solfainge songes of v; vj: vij & viij pts'. Parsons was a gentleman of the Chapel Royal from 1563. In this piece the 'in nomine' itself appears in the treble part at the bottom right of the opening.
Add. MS 31390, ff.24v, 25.
390 × 560 mm.

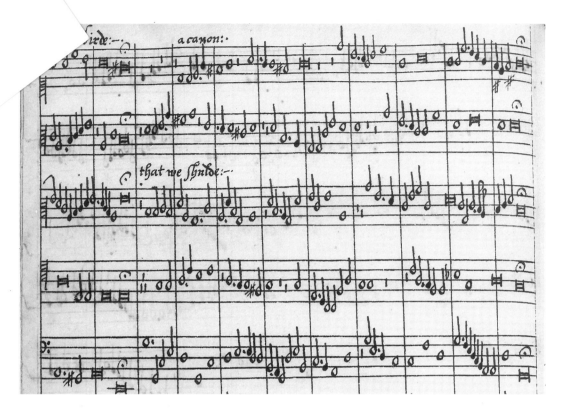

16 William Byrd (1543–1623): The 'Great Service'
An extract from the *Te Deum*, from the most important of Byrd's settings of the Anglican liturgy. It was copied in score shortly after 1600 in the commonplace book of John Baldwin, a gentleman of the Chapel Royal. His purpose seems to have been musical study, since only occasional phrases from the words are given.
R.M. 24.d.2., f.83v.

17 Thomas Tallis (*c.* 1505–1585): Motet 'Sing and glorify' ('Spem in alium')
This manuscript is the earliest surviving source for

the work, and can be dated to *c.* 1610, since it sets English words used in the ceremonies marking the creation of Prince Henry, the eldest son of James I, as Prince of Wales. Henry died in 1612. The name of his younger brother Charles has been inserted beside his (see detail below), suggesting that Tallis's music was used again in 1616, when Charles (the future Charles I) was in his turn created Prince of Wales. Before the music, on the first page of the manuscript, both the English text and the original Latin are written out.
Egerton MS 3512, ff.5v, 6. 790 × 570 mm.

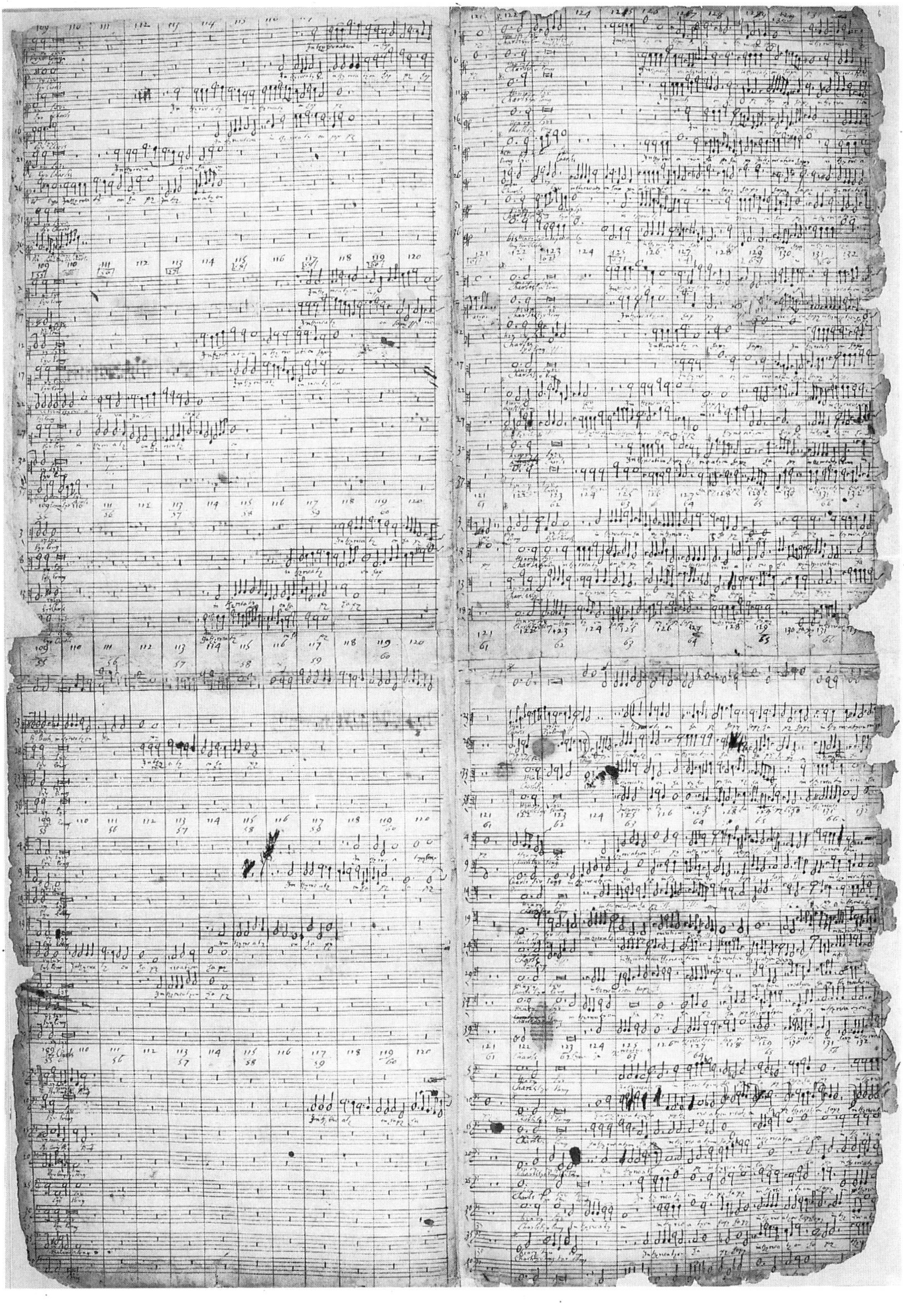

18 Orlando Gibbons (1583–1625): 'The Cries of London' A consort song, for the entertainment of five singers and five viol players. It is perhaps not surprising that there are variants to the words in a number of sources. This is the alto from a set of part-books dated 1616, made up of pieces collected by Thomas Myriell under the title *Tristitiae Remedium*.

Add. MS 29373, ff. 33v, 34. 303 × 390 mm.

19 'The Willow Song' A setting with lute accompaniment (written out in tablature) of the popular song beginning 'The poor soul sat sighing by a sycamore tree' which Shakespeare gave to Desdemona in Act IV of *Othello*. The tune in this manuscript, of 1616 or earlier, is probably the one Shakespeare knew.

Add. MS 15117, f. 18. 298 × 195 mm.

The poore Sule sate syghinge by a Sickamore tree, Singe willo, willo, willo

wt his hand in his bosom & his heade vpon his knee o willo willo :/: willo O willo willo

willo willo, Sall be my garland Singe all a greene willo, willo willo willo, Aye me by

greene willo, must be my garland

He sight in his singinge and made a great moane, I si
I am deade to all pleasure, my treue love she is gone, Sy
The mute birde sate by him, was made tame by his mones,
The treue teares fell from him woulde have melted ye stones.

Com all ye forsaken, & mourne yt wt mee,
who speakes of a false love, myne falser then shee, Singe

Let love no more boast her, in pallas nor bower,
it buddes but it blasteth, ere it be a flower. Singe

Thos fain, more false, I dye wth they wounds,
Sgaros hath lost the truest lover that goes vpp the grownd. S

Let nobody blayde her, her scornes I approue,
shee was borne to be false, and I to dye for love. Singe

Take this for my farewell and latest adewe,
write this on my tombe, that in love I was trewe. Singe

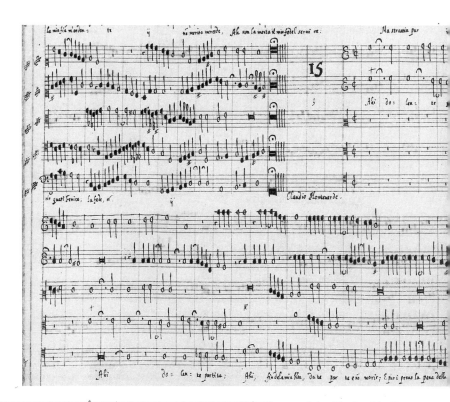

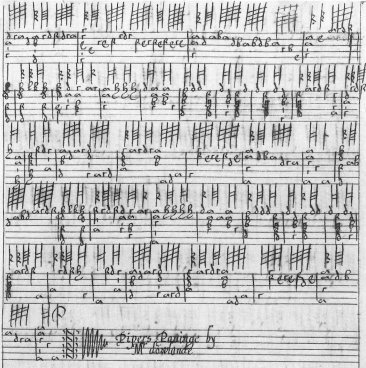

20 John Dowland (1563–1626): Piper's Pavan
A page from the late sixteenth-century lute book of Jane Pickering, written in French tablature. In the way in which he signed himself in a friend's autograph album in Germany in the 1590s (*right*), Dowland acknowledged *Lachrymae* as his most popular piece of all; above his signature he wrote a little canon on the opening notes of the Lord's Prayer in the English Protestant psalter.
Egerton MS 2046, f.20; Add. MS 27579, f.88.

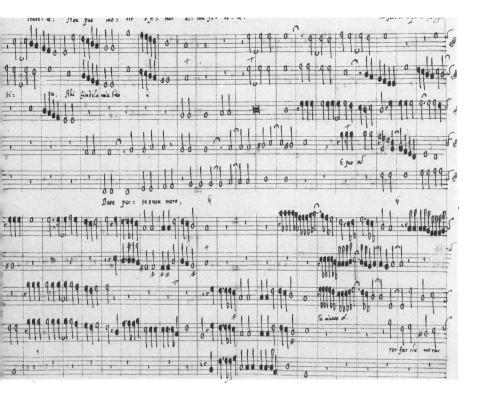

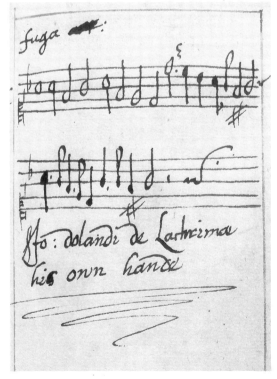

21 The Tregian Anthology: Monteverdi, madrigal 'Ahi dolente partita'

Part of an opening from the section devoted to five-part vocal works in the manuscript compilation assembled by Francis Tregian (1574–1619). Tregian wrote the music across both pages of each opening of the volume. The piece is from Monteverdi's Fourth Book of Madrigals, published in 1603.

Egerton MS 3665, ff.209v, 210. Width of opening, 710 mm.

1.

Ayre.

Couranto

2

From the later 17th Century to Schubert

Charles II was crowned on St George's day 1661. On the previous day he had gone by water to the Tower of London and from there processed through the City to Whitehall. Three great triumphal arches spanned his route, and 'entertainments' in music and verse were given at various points. At the second triumphal arch, in Cornhill, the king's own wind band played. Matthew Locke's music 'For his Majestys Sagbutts & Cornetts' (**22**) is traditionally associated with this occasion, and the city

Henry Lawes: portrait engraved by William Faithorne.
Add. MS 53723, f.viii.

22 Matthew Locke (1622–1677): music 'For his Majestys Sagbutts & Cornetts', 1661
The first of the suite of pieces written by Locke at the time of the coronation of Charles II, from the large folio volume in which the composer copied many of his works. The early nineteenth-century annotation is by the harpist and musical antiquary Edward Jones.
Add. MS 17801, f.62. *Autograph.* 420 × 270 mm.

23 Henry Lawes (1596–1662): song 'From ye Heav'ns now I flye', from *Comus*, 1634
The first of the five songs for Milton's masque in the volume of well over 300 songs which Lawes compiled by stages through most of his creative life. As he has noted, *Comus* was performed at Ludlow Castle in 1634.
Add. MS 53723, f.37. *Autograph.* 375 × 248 mm.

accounts confirm his prominent role in the celebrations. At the Restoration in 1660 Locke had been appointed Composer in Ordinary to the king for the wind music, and for the 24 'Violins of the King' with which Charles sought to emulate the musical establishment at the court of France, where he had spent much of his period of exile.

Locke also wrote music for the theatre, where he took up the masque, a form which had been popular at court before the civil war, and developed it in directions which paved the way for the stage works of Purcell. Milton's *Comus* is a rare private and provincial example of the earlier masque, not least because the music, written by the singer and composer Henry Lawes, survives (23). The music of Lawes, of his younger brother William, and of Locke gives some idea of the conditions in which Purcell's supreme genius flowered; he is represented here by the anthem which he wrote for the coronation of James II (25).

Purcell's court odes and anthems draw on the English choral tradition in ways which were followed and further developed by Handel, notably in 'Zadok the priest' and the other anthems he wrote for the coronation of George II in 1727. *Messiah* (30) is a quintessentially English work, even though it was written for Dublin and first performed there in 1742. By the time that he wrote it, Handel had been a naturalised British subject for many years, but he remains the most striking example of the contribution made to English musical life by resident or visiting foreign musicians. For his opera seasons he imported Italian singers to perform beside their English colleagues. Later in the century J. C. Bach became the 'London' Bach, and established an important series of concerts with the composer and viola da gamba player Carl Friedrich Abel. In the years 1791–5 concert giving in London was revitalised by the visits of Joseph Haydn – at the invitation of the violinist and impresario Johann Peter Salomon, a Rhinelander by birth. The 'Drum Roll' symphony (32) is the eleventh of the twelve Haydn wrote for these London concerts. The performances of Handel oratorios which he heard in England at this time were to have a direct influence on his later work.

After the success of Salomon's enterprise, a number of subsequent concert series set out to explore further the new European, and especially Viennese, music, adding Mozart and Beethoven to the repertory. The most successful (and longest lasting) was the Philharmonic Society, established in 1813 with Salomon as one of its founder members. It was another founder member of the Philharmonic, Sir George Smart, who arranged for Weber to come to London in 1826. His last opera, *Oberon*, was written for Covent Garden, and Weber died in London that same year, at Smart's house, not long after he had conducted the first performances. He was also a brilliant pianist, and his C major piano concerto is shown here (38).

Haydn was the senior of the three great Viennese composers, and his considerable influence on the other two is to some extent documented in the British Library's manuscript collections. They include the autograph scores of the six string quartets which Mozart wrote in 1782–5 (35), and published with a dedication to Haydn (24). The presence of Haydn in

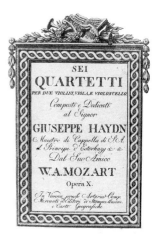

24 The title page of the first edition of Mozart's 'Haydn' quartets, 1785.
R.M. 11.g.17.(1).

25 Henry Purcell (1659–1695): anthem 'My heart is inditing', 1685
An anthem for double choir and strings, written for the coronation of James II. Purcell was a gentleman of the Chapel Royal from 1682.

R.M. 20.h.8., f.57. *Autograph.* 410 × 250 mm.

26 Agostino Steffani (1654–1728): duet 'E perchè non m'uccidete'

One of the elegant chamber duets which form the cornerstone of Steffani's musical output. After his appointment in 1709 as Apostolic Vicar in North Germany (he was an ordained priest), Steffani increasingly neglected composition to concentrate on diplomatic affairs.

R.M. 23.k.14., f.43v. *Autograph.* 170 × 225 mm.

Vienna was one of the factors which determined the young Beethoven to go there, and he recorded the payments for his first lessons from the older composer in a little notebook which is now in the Library, as are his sketches for the 'Pastoral' symphony (37).

Handel had first been invited to London in 1710, to help establish Italian *opera seria*; indeed, his success confirmed the change in taste since Purcell's day. This operatic form dominated the theatres of Europe for most of the century. The example chosen here is Alessandro Scarlatti's *La Griselda* (27), written for the Marchese Ruspoli and performed in Rome in 1721. The music in eighteenth-century opera was frequently fashioned to display the abilities of particular singers, and the aria illustrated was inserted into the score by Scarlatti for the castrato Carestini, a replacement member of the cast and a new singer who made his debut in this opera. Immediately before he came to England Handel had been in Rome, where he met Alessandro Scarlatti and his son Domenico, and numbered the Ruspoli among his patrons; in the 1730s he engaged Carestini to sing in London.

Thomas Arne was among the exponents of rival forms of opera in England; the masque *Alfred* includes 'Rule Britannia'. His arrangement of 'God Save the King' for the Drury Lane theatre is shown here (34). In his

27 Alessandro Scarlatti (1660–1725): opera *La Griselda*, 1721
The aria 'Godi bell' alma, godi rallegrati', which Scarlatti wrote for the castrato singer Carestini. There are long passages of brilliant coloratura, and one bar is left blank to indicate the insertion of a vocal cadenza.
Add. MS 14168, f.43. *Autograph.* 210 × 280 mm.

works of the 1760s and 1770s Gluck succeeded in reforming the elaborate conventions of *opera seria* from within, rather than resorting to alternatives. His 'reform' operas, mostly on classical subjects, have more direct drama, greater flexibility of musical form, and avoid excess of vocal display. *Alceste* (**29**) was the second of these works, and Gluck chose the preface to the published score to declare his aims. But 'unreformed' Italian opera persisted amid the evolution of other forms; Mozart's *La Clemenza di Tito* demonstrates that the framework of the old tradition could still support great music. *Clemenza* stands beside *Die Zauberflöte* in the entries for 1791 in Mozart's catalogue of his own works (**36**), and he has carefully noted the names of the singers at the first performance in Prague.

All but one of the manuscripts in this section are autograph. The exception is the work by Domenico Scarlatti, who left Italy to spend the greater part of his creative life in Portugal and Spain. Like his father, he wrote operas as well as cantatas and sacred music, but he is best known today for his keyboard sonatas. None of these survives in Scarlatti's own handwriting; the manuscript here was copied out in the late 1740s for one of the organists in the Spanish royal chapel (**31**), so was written in Spain during the composer's lifetime. It is a unique source for a number of the 44 sonatas it contains.

Fuga ex Moll. à 4. di J. S. Bach

32

28 Johann Sebastian Bach (1685–1750); fugue in A flat major from Book II of *Das Wohltemperirte Clavier*
This manuscript, written out by Bach at some time between 1740 and 1742, contains 21 of the 24 fugues from the second book. Most, like this, are in Bach's hand alone; in others he had the help of his second wife Anna Magdalena.
Add. MS 35021, f.14. *Autograph.* 318 × 202 mm.

The differences in purpose and appearance between the Lawes, Locke and Purcell anthology volumes and the manuscripts of J. S. Bach, Handel and Mozart are discussed in the general introduction (p. 7 above). Though written out in haste, the manuscript of the aria from the opera by Alessandro Scarlatti is intended for use in performance, just as is the Bach manuscript (**28**). The Venetian Agostino Steffani, another opera composer, studied in Rome, as Domenico Scarlatti and Handel had done, and also subsequently became a musical exile. The chamber duet shown here (**26**) is among those he revised in 1702–3, while he was Kapellmeister at the Hanoverian court; having been written out in this elegant form for presentation, the manuscript passed into the English royal collection with others from Hanover.

29 Christoph Willibald Gluck (1714–1787): aria 'Misero! E che faro' from the opera *Alceste*, 1767
The aria from Act III for the character Admeto (a tenor role) is here written out by Gluck in the soprano clef, and with a slightly reduced orchestra from that used in the score for the first performances of the work in Vienna in 1767. Gluck revised the opera for Paris in 1776.
Zweig MS 34, f.4v. *Autograph.* 226 × 310 mm.

30 George Frideric Handel (1685–1759): *Messiah*, 1742 Part of the soprano aria 'O thou that tellest good tidings to Zion' and of the 'Halleluiah' chorus. The text for *Messiah* was compiled from the bible and the psalms as they appear in the English prayer book, by Charles Jennens, a country gentleman of literary tastes and with a great admiration for Handel's music. R.M. 20.f.2., ff.25, 103v. *Autograph.* 238 × 295 mm.

31 Domenico Scarlatti (1685–1757): sonata for harpsichord in C major, K.143
One of the sonatas for which this Spanish manuscript is the only source. The manuscript was acquired before 1752 by an English musician who had been inspired with a love of Scarlatti's music by the Irish-born composer Thomas Roseingrave. Roseingrave had met Domenico, and heard him play, in Italy in 1710.
Add. MS 31553, f.83v. 262 × 350 mm.

The piano sonata by Schubert (**39**) is the manuscript prepared by the composer for the printer, and the engraver's tiny markings of the points where the lines in his copying end are to be found at the bottom of the lines of music. Even so, it contains a number of autograph alterations, in addition to erased portions of an earlier version of the slow movement. By far the most striking visual evidence of a composer at work, though, is found in Beethoven's sketches for the 'Pastoral' Symphony (**37**). This page from one of a number of his sketchbooks in the Library shows the evolution of musical ideas now familiar from the finished work.

32 Joseph Haydn (1732–1809): symphony no. 103 in E flat major, the 'Drum Roll', 1795

The name comes from the roll on the timpani with which the symphony's slow introduction begins. These pages show the end of that section and the beginning of the Allegro.

Add. MS 31707, ff.3v–4. *Autograph.* 242 × 600 mm.

33 Haydn's signature on a receipt dated 12 February 1802 for payment from the Edinburgh music publisher George Thompson, for whom he made arrangements of British folk-songs. Haydn had been given the degree of honorary doctor of music by the University of Oxford in 1792.

Add. MS 35263, f.142.

34 Thomas Augustine Arne
(1710–1778): 'God bless our
noble King', arranged for
voices and instruments, 1745.
Add. MS 29370, f.114. *Autograph.*

35 *page 38* Wolfgang Amadeus Mozart (1756–1791): string quartet in
G major, K.387, 1782
The opening of the slow movement of the first of Mozart's six 'Haydn'
string quartets. The instructions written in the margin concern copying
the parts and include 'Die Bass stimme kommt erst nach tisch': the bass
part is to be copied after dinner.
Add. MS 37763, f.6v. *Autograph.* 232 × 318 mm.

38

36 Wolfgang Amadeus Mozart (1756–1791): 'Verzeichnüss aller meiner Werke . . .'
The last pages, for July–November 1791, from the little catalogue in which Mozart entered details of his
compositions from 1784 until his death. At the top *La Clemenza di Tito* appears between two entries for *Die
Zauberflöte*. The page ends with Mozart's last completed work, the Masonic Cantata K.623.
Zweig MS 63, ff. 28v,29. Autograph. 215 × 326 mm.

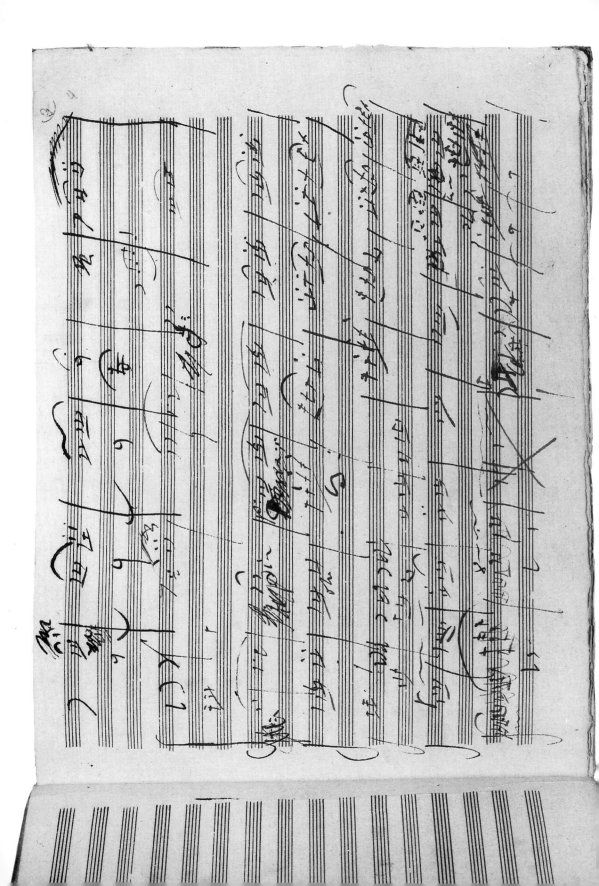

37 Ludwig van Beethoven (1770–1827): sketches for symphony no. 6 in F major, op. 68, the 'Pastoral', 1808

These sketches for part of the first movement give occasional indications of instrumentation, such as 'obo', 'clari'. This sketchbook also includes material for the two piano trios op. 70, nos. 1 and 2, composed in the same year.

Add. MS 31766, f.4. *Autograph.* 235 × 300 mm.

38 Carl Maria von Weber (1786–1826): piano concerto no. 1 in C major, 1810

The opening of slow movement. The imaginative and atmospheric scoring, for two horns, timpani, solo viola, two cellos, and double bass, is no less characteristic than the bravura display of the solo part in the outer movements.

Add. MS 47853, f.18. *Autograph.* 242 × 335 mm.

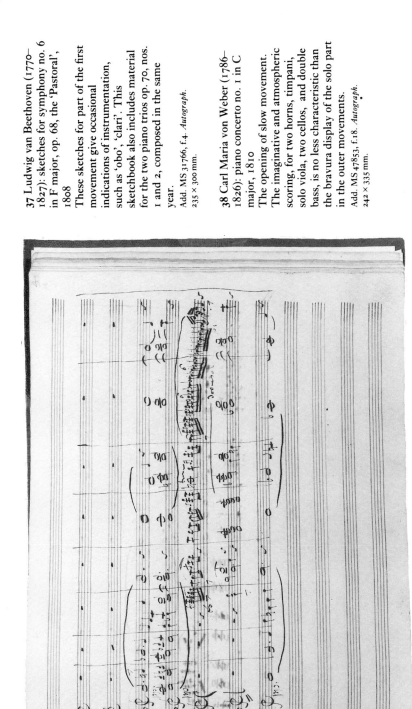

39 Franz Schubert (1797–1828): piano sonata in G major, D.894, 1826
The opening of the Andante. Part of the cancelled earlier version of this movement can be seen on the facing page. Schubert composed the sonata in October 1826, and it was published the following year as op. 78. Few of his piano works were published in his lifetime.
Add. MS 36738, f.7. *Autograph.*
250 × 320 mm.

From Chopin to Brahms

A reception given for Liszt at Grosvenor House, London, on 8 April, 1886. Among those present were the violinist Joachim and Sir Arthur Sullivan.

Add. MS 35027, f.79

The piano sonatas of the great Viennese composers of the early years of the nineteenth century were written for a new instrument, still subject to technical development. Schubert was particularly aware of its possibilities in freer and often shorter forms. These technical and formal developments were pursued by the later nineteenth-century pianist-composers. Although Chopin designed pieces like the Mazurka (40) for the salon, or even the parlour, he managed to create a whole new emotional range for the instrument as well as to extend the player's technique. Mendelssohn's piano music is more obviously domestic, never more so than in the duet versions of the *Songs without Words* which he made for Victoria and Albert (45), the royal couple who set the standard of family life for a whole empire. Liszt designed most of his original compositions for the piano for his own use in recitals, either in public or before the great families of Europe, so that many of them require a prodigious technique. His concert fantasias and paraphrases on the works of others often served the same purpose, like his late, and harmonically adventurous *Réminiscences* of Verdi's *Simon Boccanegra* (47). But he also wrote relatively straight-forward transcriptions (of all the Beethoven symphonies, for example) to make works accessible through the medium of the piano, either because they were seldom performed otherwise, or for the benefit of music lovers who had no opportunity to attend concerts.

Schumann used the piano to express his most personal feelings, even in longer works. The manuscript of the F minor sonata (42) is full of corrections and second thoughts, and he remained undecided about the form the

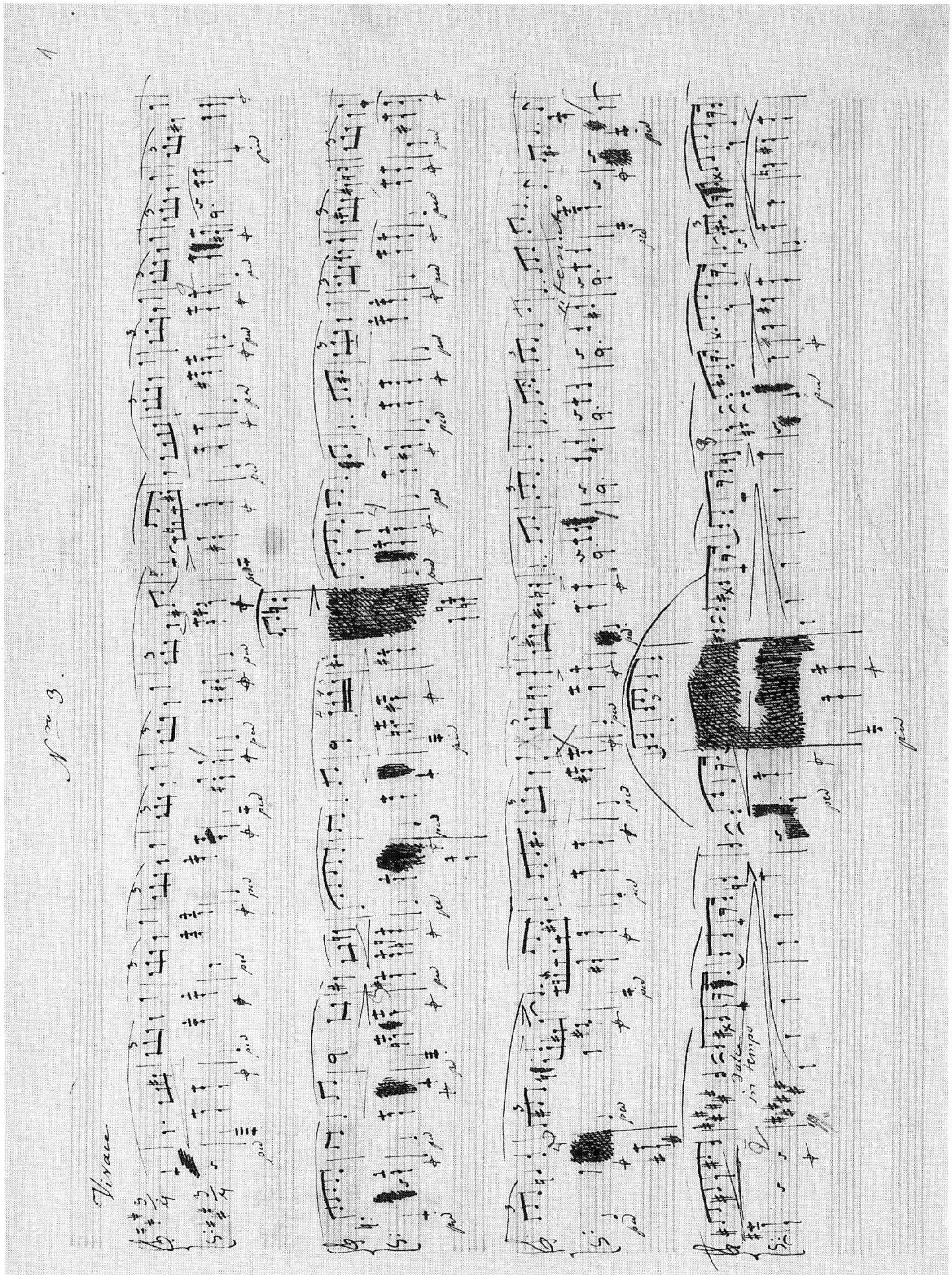
N° 3.
Vivace

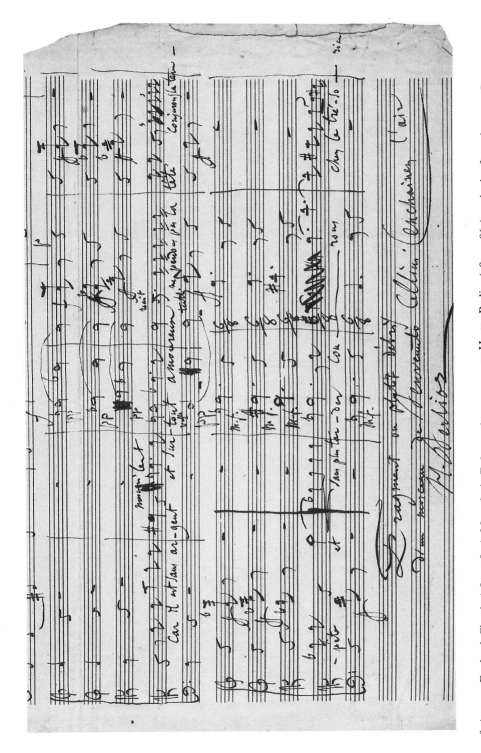

40 *facing page* Fryderyk Chopin (1810–1849): Mazurka in F sharp minor,
op. 59, no. 3

Many of Chopin's shorter piano pieces were written for his pupils. In his
mazurkas he adopted the form of one of the country dances of his native
Poland; this one dates from 1845.

Zweig MS 26, f.1. *Autograph*. 220 × 280 mm.

41 Hector Berlioz (1803–1869): recitative from the opera *Benvenuto
Cellini*

The opera was composed 1834–7. This recitative does not appear in the
final work, and Berlioz presumably added his dismissive comment when
the leaf was discarded.

Loan 91.2. *Autograph*.

42 *left* Robert Schumann (1810–1856): Sonata in F minor, op. 14, 1836 Written at the time that Schumann fell in love with his future wife, Clara, whose family at first opposed the match. The 'Quasi Variazioni' movement is based on a 'Melodie de Clara Wieck'.
Add. MS 37056, f.15v.
Autograph. 266 × 340 mm.

43 *right* Gioachino Rossini (1792–1868): 'Stabat Mater' The tenor solo 'Cuius animam' is one of the four numbers of the 'Stabat Mater' which Rossini composed in 1841. He had written the other six to a commission in 1832, but only the appearance of a pirate edition which included them induced him to complete his own setting.

Add. MS 43970, f.17v. *Autograph.* 220 × 282 mm.

44 *below* Gaetano Donizetti (1797–1848): duet 'Se lontan ben mio tu sei' From an undated manuscript of three vocal duets, dedicated to Nina Rovetti. The name Nina appears among the doodles and symbols of suffering with which Donizetti has embellished the page.

Loan 91.1. *Autograph.* 223 × 320 mm.

work should have: it was first published as a 'Concert pour piano seul' omitting the two Scherzo movements to be found in the manuscript, then republished as a sonata with one of the Scherzos reinstated. The other Scherzo was published by Brahms in 1866. In his own music Brahms explored the sonorities of the piano almost to the end of the century: the E flat Rhapsody (57) belongs to the last group of solo pieces he published.

A remarkable generation of composers was born in Russia in the 1830s and 1840s. Chaikovsky was the most immediately successful abroad, perhaps because he was the least obviously nationalistic. His letter to the Philharmonic Society of London (50) is a reminder of the English musical establishment's continued reliance on foreign musicians. (One of Mendelssohn's English links has already been mentioned; he also conducted his own works for the Philharmonic, as did Berlioz and Wagner.) Musorgsky's music, much more Russian in feeling than that of Chaikovsky, had a delayed impact in the West. As a result the manuscript of two of his song settings, one of a translation into Russian of words by Goethe (46), is one of the few to be found outside his native country. Borodin carried the manuscript of his *Petite Suite* with him on a journey round Europe in 1885, correcting the printer's proofs for publication while he travelled. He played the pieces to Liszt in Weimar, and subsequently gave his pencil draft (48) to some Belgian friends in gratitude for their hospitality.

Piano music is one thread which unites the manuscripts here; opera is another. Berlioz was always drawn to dramatic subjects, as the titles of all

45 Felix Mendelssohn-Bartholdy (1809–1847): 'Spring Song'
This piano duet arrangement of 'Frühlingslied' from the *Songs without Words*, op. 62, was made by Mendelssohn especially for Queen Victoria and Prince Albert. He presented the manuscript to them in 1844.
R.M. 21.f.24.(5.), ff.10v, 11.
Autograph. 330 × 500 mm.

46 Modest Musorgsky
(1839–1881): song 'Iz slez
moikh' ('From my Tears'),
1866
This manuscript has a
number of variants from the
(posthumously) published
version. It is written out with
a second song composed in
the same year.
Zweig MS 70, f.4. *Autograph.*
260 × 378 mm.

of his symphonic works demonstrate. *Benvenuto Cellini* (**41**), his first opera
to be produced, was initially a dismal failure with audiences, but it at last
brought his peculiar genius for melody and orchestration to the theatre. It
was first performed in 1838, a year before Verdi's first opera was heard; his
ninth, *Attila* (**52**), was staged in Venice in 1846. By that time Verdi was in
demand in all the major theatres of Italy, even though his greatest works
were to come.

Verdi brought a dramatic vitality to Italy's strong operatic tradition
which ensured his early success. Two of the main contributors to that
tradition, Rossini and Donizetti, are represented here by vocal works from
other fields (**43**, **44**). Both, though, were prolific opera composers, who
exploited the coloratura technique which singers had developed since the
eighteenth century. Rossini was able to convey a range of emotion within
existing musical forms, resulting in an apparent discrepancy between text
and music which made it difficult for audiences in the first part of the
present century to accept his serious operas. During the same period
musical taste turned away from his setting of the thirteenth-century devo-
tional poem 'Stabat Mater' (**43**), though it had a huge initial success, and
its musical and emotional warmth are appreciated again now.

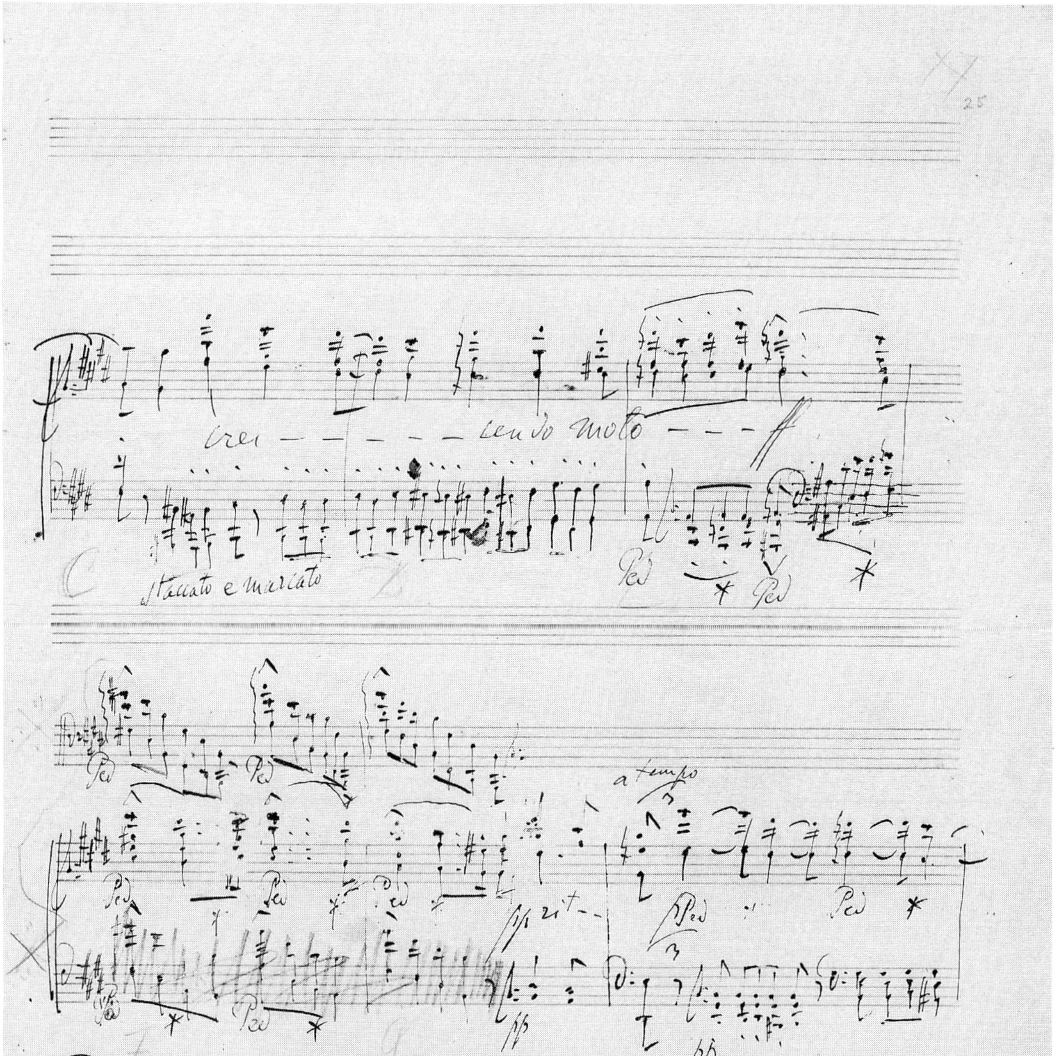
25
cre - - - - - scendo molto - - -
ff
staccato e marcato
Ped
a tempo
rit
pp

47 Franz Liszt (1811–1886): *Réminiscences de Simone Boccanegra*, 1882
Liszt wrote transcriptions and 'paraphrases' of the music of other composers from Bach to those of his own day as well as original works for piano throughout his career. He drew on six other Verdi operas in addition to *Boccanegra*, and also arranged part of the Requiem.

Egerton MS 2735, f.25. *Autograph.* 342 × 268 mm.

48 Alexander Borodin (1833–1887): *Petite Suite* for piano, 1885
Though slight pieces, these are works of Borodin's maturity. The short 'Reverie' conjures up the world of the slow movement of his second string quartet.

Egerton MS 3087, f.2. *Autograph.* 180 × 225 mm.

49 Antonín Dvořák (1841–1904): Cello concerto in A major, 1865
This concerto is among the earliest of Dvorak's serious works. Despite
the lyrical quality and opportunities for bravura display in the solo part,
he left the work in this form for cello and piano. Orchestral versions were
made only after his death.

Add. MS 42050, f.28. *Autograph.* 310 × 247 mm.

50 Petr Il'ich Chaikovsky (1840–1893): letter to the Philharmonic Society of London, 16 January, 1893 Chaikovsky writes from Paris – in German – arranging to give his Symphony no.4 with the Society. He conducted the first British performance at the Philharmonic concert on 1 June 1893.

Loan 48.13/34, f.164. *Autograph*.

Like Berlioz, Wagner had to struggle to gain an audience for the kind of opera he felt impelled to create. *The Flying Dutchman*, written in 1842, is the earliest of his operas to have remained in the repertory. When Wagner's fortunes were at a low ebb in 1860–1 he turned to it again. By that time he had composed much of *The Ring* and completed *Tristan and Isolde*, and yet in 1861 *Tannhäuser* was forced off the stage in Paris. His revisions to *The Flying Dutchman* in 1860 included a new ending to the overture (**51**) prepared for a Paris concert.

Comic opera in Paris in the 1860s was provided by Jacques Offenbach, himself German in origin. *La Belle Hélène* (**53**), like *Orpheus in the Underworld*, is a commentary on contemporary society and politics under cover of a spoof of the classical story. Allowing for obvious differences of national temperament, the Savoy Operas of Gilbert and Sullivan (**54**) performed much the same function; their first successful collaboration, *Trial by Jury*, was specifically written to be performed with Offenbach's *La Périchole*.

51 Richard Wagner (1813–1883): Overture to *Der Fliegende Holländer*.

The revised ending of the overture written in Paris in 1860. Wagner wrote out this manuscript to send to his copyist in Germany, and the section shown here incorporates the opera's best known theme.

Zweig MS 116, p.8. *Autograph.* 330 × 250 mm.

52 Giuseppe Verdi (1813–1901): *Attila*, 1846

The cabaletta to Odabella's aria in the Prologue. After completing the score, Verdi re-wrote the vocal line for the soprano Sofia Loewe; he also intended the role of Lady Macbeth in his next opera for her. The score is written with the upper strings at the top of the page.

Add. MS 35156, f.55. *Autograph.* 325 × 230 mm.

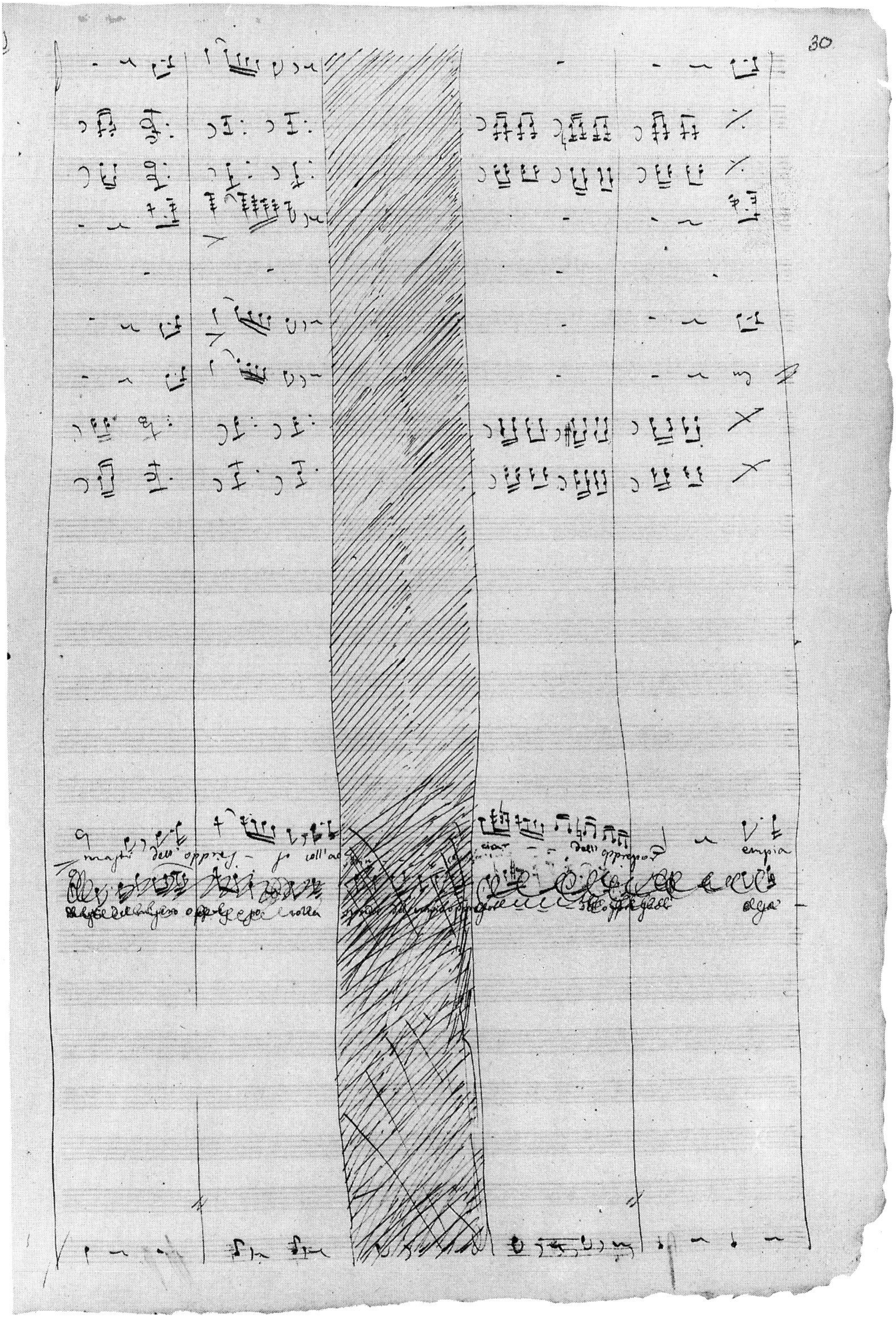
30
empia

53 Jacques
Offenbach (1819–
1880): *La Belle
Hélène*, 1864
The 'Trio
Patriotique' in the
final act, in which
Agamemnon and
Calchas round on
King Menelas with
the words 'Lorsque
la Grece est un
champ de carnage,
Quand on immole
les maris, Tu vis
heureux au sein de
ton ménage . . .'.
Zweig MS 72, f.169.
Autograph.
263 × 336 mm.

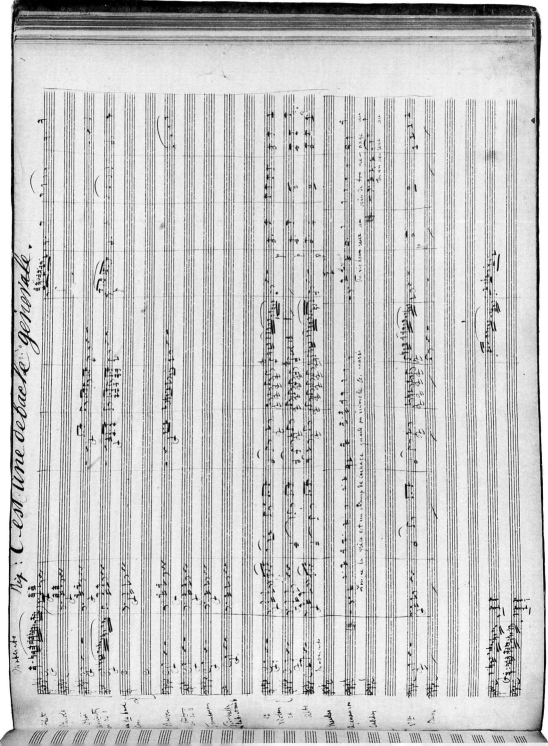

54 Sir Arthur
Sullivan (1842–
1900): *The
Gondoliers*, 1889
The Duke of Plaza-
Toro's song 'I am a
courtier grave and
serious' from Act
II, in which he
attempts to explain
court etiquette to
the two gondoliers.
Add. MS 53779, f.195.
Autograph.
265 × 335 mm.

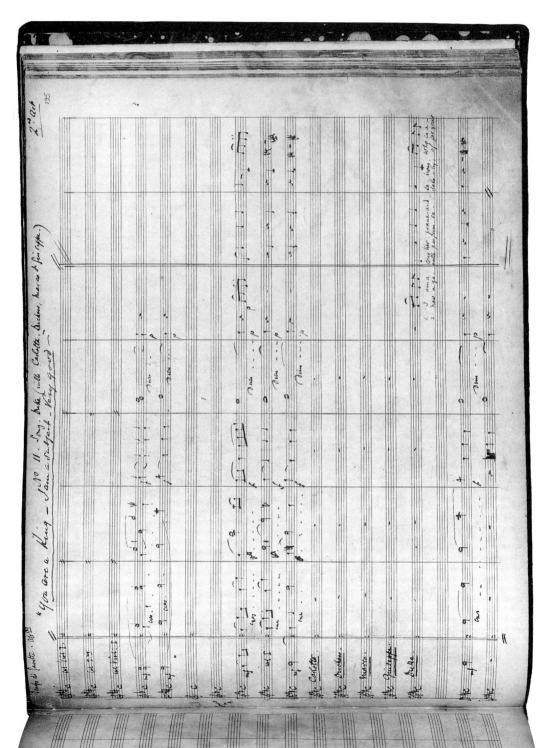

4. Solvejgs Lied.
Solvejgs Sang.

Gesang Weyla's.

55 Edvard Grieg (1843–1907): *Peer Gynt* Suite
no.2, 1891
'Solvieg's Song', the final number in the suite.
Grieg made his two orchestral suites from
incidental music he had written for Ibsen's play in
1876.

Zweig MS 35, p.51. Autograph. 338 × 262 mm.

56 Hugo Wolf (1860–1903): 'Gesang Weylas',
1888
One of the 53 settings of words by the Swabian
poet Eduard Mörike which Wolf composed in
1888 and 1889. Altogether Wolf wrote over 300
songs for voice and piano, developing great
sensitivity to the words he set.

Zweig MS 130. *Autograph.* 345 × 265 mm.

57 Johannes Brahms (1833–
1897): Rhapsody in E flat
major for piano, op.119, no.4,
1893
The end of the middle section
of the Rhapsody, and the
return to the main theme.
This manuscript, which
Brahms wrote out for Clara
Schumann, is the only
surviving autograph of the
piece.
Add. MS 41866, f.3v. *Autograph.*
266 × 325 mm.

Debussy, Mahler and the 20th Century

The manuscripts in this section span over 80 years, and at the centre of that period lies the one work among them which is actually written following the twelve-note method of composition, Berg's opera *Lulu* (**65**). The development and employment of serial technique, first by Schoenberg (**63**), then by Webern (**64**) and Berg, has become the text-book example of the radical changes which have fragmented music in the twentieth century. There are many different apparently conflicting or unrelated trends, and a comprehensive view is scarcely possible.

The examples given here illustrate the diversity of twentieth-century music; they also provide a reminder of some unexpected links, and of the ways in which the careers of composers who appear quite distinct actually overlap. Debussy's 'Fantaisie' for piano and orchestra of 1890 (**58**) is the last of the three works which it was his duty to write as a recipient of the Prix de Rome. Following a dispute during rehearsals the first performance was cancelled, and Debussy would not then allow public performance or publication during his lifetime. Nonetheless, it is a serious large-scale piece, written before the Mahler and Elgar works.

'Urlicht' (**61**) is one of a number of settings which Mahler made from

Sir Adrian Boult, Ralph Vaughan Williams (seated), and Sir Henry Wood.
Add. MS 56443 A, f.29

Das Knaben Wunderhorn, an anthology of German folk poetry; he incorporated this particular setting into his second symphony. Elgar's *Enigma* Variations (**62**) date from 1899, the year before *The Dream of Gerontius*, a work which Richard Strauss heard and praised at the Lower Rhine Festival in 1902. Strauss was already an internationally established figure, and his opinion meant a great deal to Elgar, who was always uneasy about the reception of his music in England. *Capriccio* (**67**), the Strauss work here, was written forty years later, during a remarkably fruitful creative period at the end of the composer's life. It takes the form of an urbane and musically enchanting discussion of the relative merits of words and music written in the darkest days of the Second World War.

It was the last opera Strauss was to complete. He had first gained success in this field with *Salome* in 1905. *Madam Butterfly* (**60**), first performed at Milan in 1904, was the third success in a row for Puccini, for it followed *La Bohème* and *Tosca*. In the first decades of the century the two composers maintained the nineteenth-century pattern of rival schools of German and Italian opera. The doubts about British audience reaction which troubled Elgar were felt more strongly by Ethel Smyth and Frederick Delius, who both had operas produced in Germany long before they reached the stage in England. Delius's *Fennimore and Gerda* (**59**) was composed in 1909–10, and staged at Frankfurt in 1919, after the First World War. By that time Stravinsky was at work on *Pulcinella* (**71**). If the juxtaposition of Delius's impressionistic opera with Stravinsky's overtly neo-classical score is provoking, the genesis of Pulcinella is bewildering: a hybrid 'ballet with song', written in Switzerland by a Russian composer, drawing on Italian music, copied out in the British Museum at the request of a Russian impresario running a ballet company in France.

Two of the composers represented here, Bartók and Vaughan Williams, were engaged in the early years of the century in collecting folk-songs in a more scientific way than the nineteenth-century nationalists had attempted. Gustav Holst, though not himself a collector, was also influenced by this movement. Vaughan Williams was most active as a collector in the years 1903–1913, hastily jotting the songs down in the small notebooks which he habitually used to record his musical ideas. The first sketch for the song 'Linden Lea' is to be found in one of these notebooks dating from a few years before he began collecting (**68**). By the time of the sixth symphony (**76**), which was composed between 1944 and 1947, Vaughan Williams had for long subsumed the influence of folk-song into his own entirely personal style. In much the same way there is no direct evidence of this influence in the Bartók and Holst works here. Both date from the time of the First World War. Bartók's Four Pieces for Orchestra (**72**) were composed in 1912, but not orchestrated until 1921. Holst was unhappy at being unfit for military service and when, at the end of the war, he volunteered to go to Salonica in an ancillary role he had only just completed work on his suite *The Planets* (**69**). Friends paid for a single private performance, conducted by Adrian Boult, on the eve of Holst's

58 Claude Debussy (1862–1918): 'Fantaisie' for piano and orchestra, 1890
The manuscript of the solo part, with a piano reduction of the orchestral passages, which Debussy prepared for rehearsals. After the cancellation of the first performance he gave this score to the pianist René Chansarel.
Zweig MS 31, f.12. *Autograph.* 345 × 265 mm.

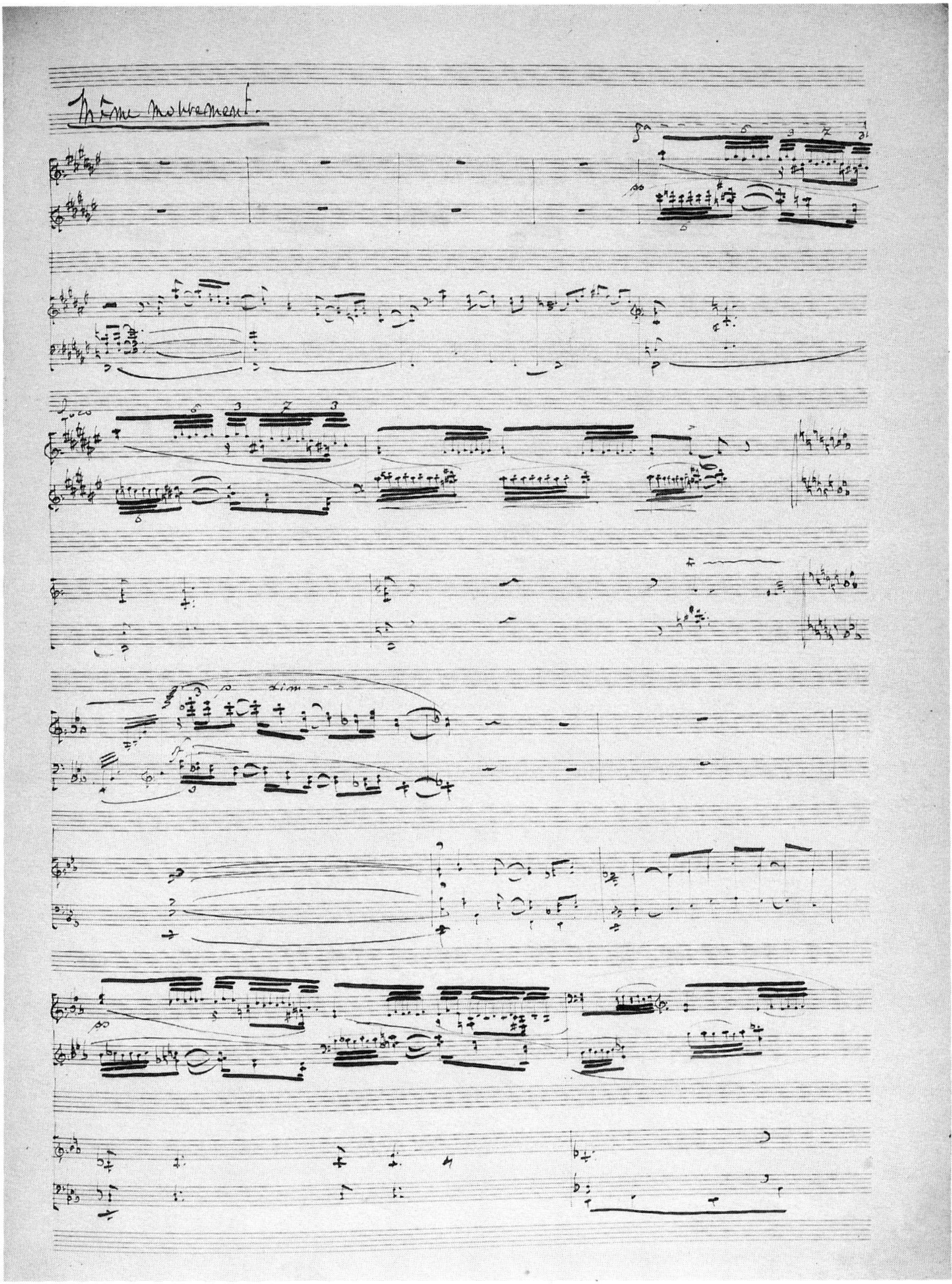
Même mouvement

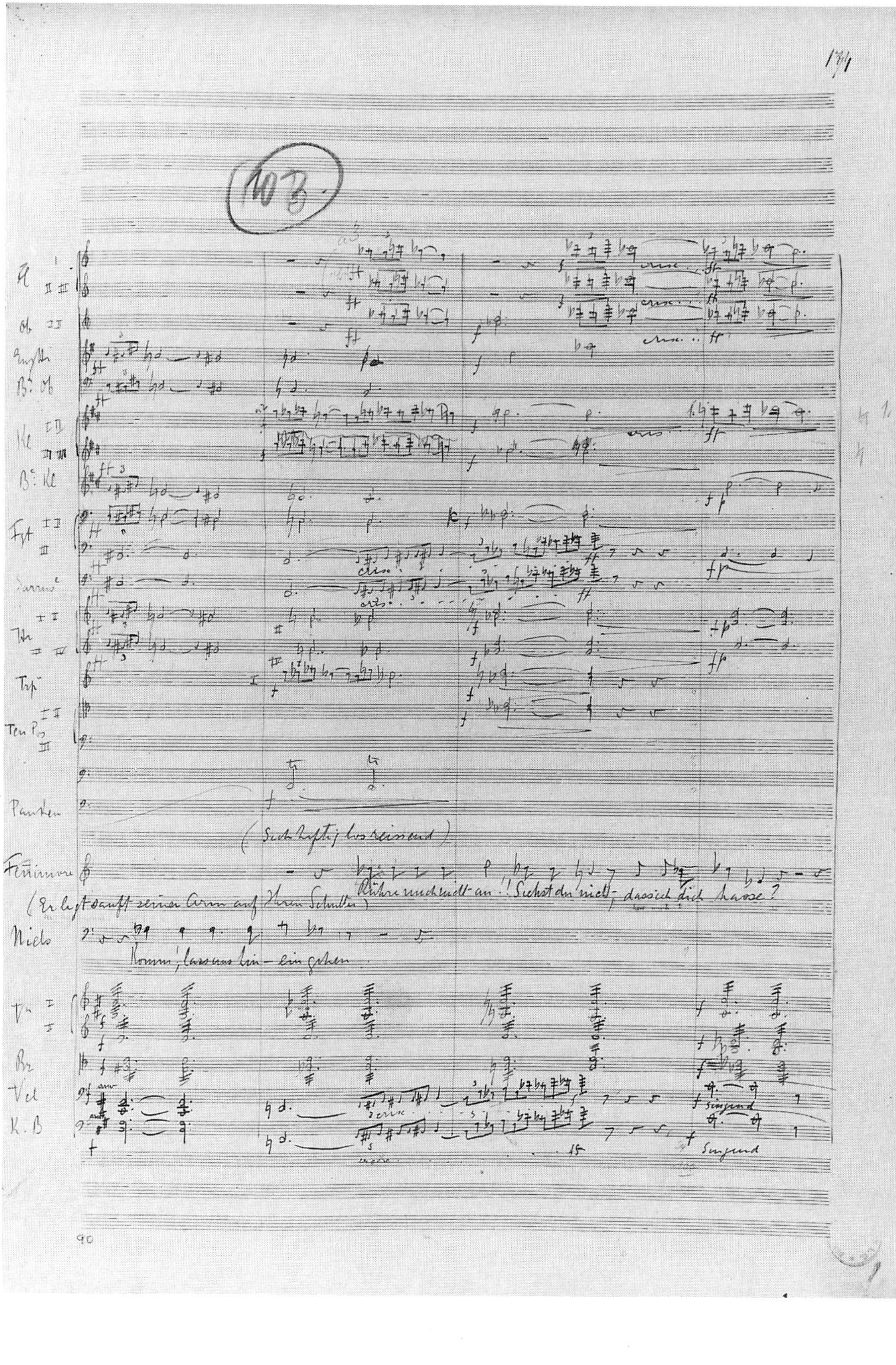

174
103
(Sich heftig losreissend)
Rühre mich nicht an! Siehst du nicht, dass ich dich hasse?
(Er legt sanft seinen Arm auf ihre Schulter)
Niels
Komm, lass uns hin-ein gehen.
Pauken

59 Frederick Delius (1862–1934): *Fennimore and Gerda*, 1909–10
A page from the composer's full score. The opera is based on an episode in J. P. Jacobsens' novel *Niels Lyhne*; this shows the point in the second scene where Niels declares his love for Fennimore. Delius made his own libretto in German and an English version was supplied by his friend Philip Heseltine (the composer 'Peter Warlock').
Loan 54.2.

60 Giacomo Puccini (1858–1924): sketch for the opera *Madama Butterfly*, 1904
The appearance of Puccini's manuscript is as dramatic as the moment in the action, at the end of the final act; as Butterfly, deserted by Pinkerton, prepares for ritual suicide, their child is thrust into the room by Suzuki, Butterfly drops the knife and embraces the child; 'Tu?. tu?, piccolo Iddio! Amore, amore mio . . .'.
Add. MS 64808, f1. *Autograph.*
333 × 257 mm.

departure, so that he was able to write to Boult with his observations and advice for the preparation of the first public performance (**70**).

Stravinsky's *Pulcinella* catches the tone of one particular strain in the music of the inter-war years. Ravel's *Boléro* (**72**) was also a ballet score in origin; the first performance took place at the Paris Opera on 22 November 1928. The brilliant and creative pastiche of Walton's *Façade* (**73**) extends to its form, which echoes that of Schoenberg's *Pierrot Lunaire*. The 'Polka' was one of the pieces introduced into the 1926 performances, which represented the fullest early version of a work which went through many stages and guises before the composer gave it authoritative form in 1951. The larger-scale works of contemporary European composers, especially of the second Viennese school, were brought to London audiences by the

61

Molto rit.
Wieder langsam wie am Anfang!
2 große Flöten
I Solo Viol.
II Solo Viol.
I Viol. Tutti
II Viol.
V.
liebe Gott! der liebe Gott, wird mir ein Lichtchen geben, wird leuchten mir bis in das

61 Gustav Mahler (1860–1911): 'Urlicht', song for contralto and orchestra, 1893
The composition score of the setting which Mahler used as the fourth movement of his 'Resurrection' Symphony. 'Urlicht' was first performed, as part of the symphony, in 1897.
Zweig MS 49, f.5v. *Autograph.* 328 × 248 mm.

62 Sir Edward Elgar (1857–1934): Variations on an Original Theme (Enigma), 1899
Elgar dedicated the work to 'my friends pictured within'. Variation 9 (the end is shown here) represents his close friend and publisher Augustus Jaeger, 'Nimrod'.
Add. MS 58004, ff.39v, 40. *Autograph.* 380 × 560 mm.

63 *page 66 above* Arnold Schoenberg (1874–1951): Five Orchestral Pieces, op. 16, 1909
Part of a page in the first of the pieces, which are among the earliest in which Schoenberg abandoned tonality.
Zweig MS 77, p.3. *Autograph.*

64 *page 66 below* Anton Webern (1883–1945): Six Pieces, op. 6, 1909
Though inspired by Schoenberg's opus 16 Pieces, Webern's have a concision typical of their composer. This funeral march (no.4) is built on a process of accumulation using a vast orchestra, Webern prepared the more familiar reduced orchestration in 1928.
Zweig MS 128, p.15. *Autograph.* 350 × 270 mm.

65 *page 67* Alban Berg (1885–1935): prologue to the opera *Lulu*, 1934
Berg began work on Lulu in 1929, but, although this manuscript includes a list of the characters in all three acts, he had not finished the orchestration of Act III when he died. The completion of his work and the first performance of the whole opera had to wait until 1979.
Zweig MS 17, f.7v. *Autograph.* 444 × 340 mm.

3me Concerto pour Piano
I
Allegro ma non tanto
J. Rachmaninoff. op. 30.
Flauti I. II.
Oboe I. II.
Clarinetti I. II
Fagotti I. II
4 Corni in F
I. II.
III. IV.
2 Trombe in B
Timpani in D. A
Piano
Violini I
Violini II
Viole
V. Celli
C. Bassi
Piano II
con sordini
comodo
dim.
№229(1) П. Юргенсонъ въ Москвѣ.

67 Richard Strauss (1864–1949): *Capriccio*, op. 85, 1940–41
Strauss's composition draft in short score of a passage from the middle of the
opera: the page begins with the last moments of scene vii, after which come the
Countess's spoken words 'Wir werden die Schokolade hier im Salon
einnehmen'. The setting of the succeeding scene is entirely different from that
eventually used.
Add. MS 52927. *Autograph*. 268 × 340 mm.

66 Sergei Rakhmaninov
(1873–1943): Piano Concerto
no.3, op. 30. 1909
Rakhmaninov was a virtuoso
pianist, and wrote this
concerto for his United States
debut in November 1909.
The manuscript full score,
like the first publication of the
work (Moscow, 1910) has, at
the foot of the page, a
reduction of the orchestra's
part for a second piano.
Loan 75.34, p.1. *Autograph*.
355 × 270 mm.

BBC, through the influence of Edward Clark and under the baton of Sir
Adrian Boult. Though Hindemith's music featured in these concerts, he
was also in demand as a solo viola player. In 1936 he was in London to play
Walton's viola concerto with Boult and the BBC orchestra. During rehearsals news came of the death of King George V. The Walton concerto was
considered unsuitable for a period of national mourning, so to replace it
Hindemith wrote in a single day his short elegy *Trauermusik* (**75**).

Benjamin Britten's Serenade for tenor, horn and strings (**77**) received
its first performance in 1943, less than a year after the première of Strauss's
Capriccio. Britten's *Peter Grimes*, first staged in 1947, marked the
beginning of an entirely new period of success for opera by English composers. Tippett's career developed more slowly than Britten's; *King Priam*
(**78**) his second opera, was performed in 1962 as part of the celebrations
marking the consecration of the new cathedral at Coventry, following the
destruction of the earlier building in the war. Britten wrote his *War
Requiem* for the same occasion.

68 Ralph Vaughan Williams (1872–1958): sketch for the song 'Linden Lea', *c.* 1901
One of the best known of all Vaughan Williams's songs. The melody appears complete in this sketch, apart from the line 'Now do quiver under foot'.
Add. MS 57294 B, ff.12v, 13. *Autograph.* 130 × 330 mm.

69 Gustav Holst (1874–1934): suite *The Planets*, 1914–17
Two piano score of Jupiter, 'the bringer of jollity'. The orchestration of this passage is marked into the score.
Add. MS 57881, f.6. *Autograph* 305 × 240 mm.

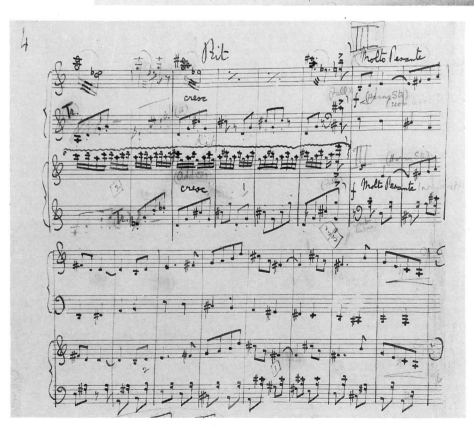

softer stops— perhaps 32 ft alone or 16 ft alone instead of both. Let it be too soft rather than too loud.

4) Jupiter. As long as he gets the wonderful joyousness you gave him he'll do. I wish you had Gryp as 1st trumpet!

At the recapitulation this part (tutti in unison)

did not come out clearly. Perhaps it should be broadened out. Do as you like.

And accept my blessing and thanks.

70 Holst's letter of 14 November 1918 to Adrian Boult, written from Salonica, commenting on the performance of *The Planets* which took place immediately before the composer left.
Add. MS 60498, f.219v.

71 Igor Stravinsky (1882–1971): sketchbook for *Pulcinella*, 1919–20
Stravinsky worked with an array of special pens and gadgets, ruling staves as required for the layout of his sketches and first drafts. These pages show linking passages between early numbers of the ballet.
Zweig MS 94, pp. 40, 41. *Autograph.* 147 × 490 mm.

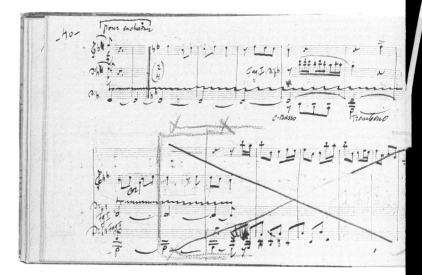

72 Béla Bartók (1881–1945): Four Pieces for Orchestra, op. 12, 1912, orchestrated 1921
The first page of the full score of no.3, Intermezzo. Bartók's fellow composer Dohnányi conducted the first performance in Budapest in 1922.
Zweig MS 5, p.63. *Autograph.* 350 × 265 mm.

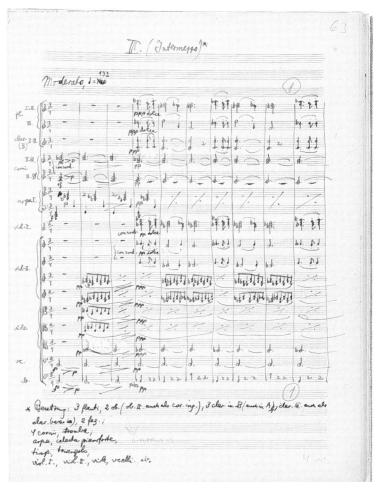

73 Sir William Walton
(1902–1983): 'Polka' from
Façade, 1926
Walton's 'entertainment' for
reciter and chamber ensemble
was first performed privately
in 1922, with the composer
conducting and Edith Sitwell
reading her poems. The Polka
was included in two
performances given in 1926.
Egerton MS 3771, f.2v. *Autograph.*
325 × 235 mm.

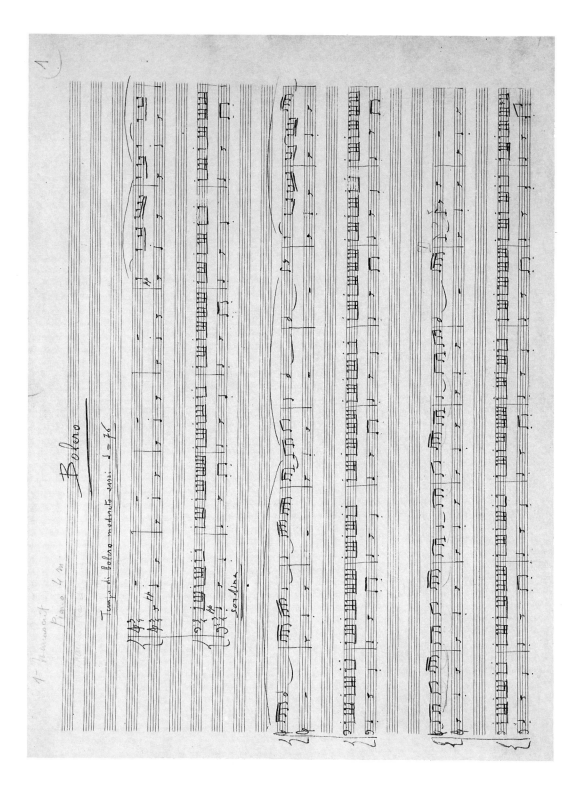

74 Maurice Ravel (1875–1937): *Boléro*, 1928
Ravel wrote *Boléro* for the dancer Ida Rubinstein, in reponse to a
request for a ballet with a Spanish flavour. Like many of his other
popular orchestral works it was published in his own arrangement for
piano duet, but the version in this manuscript differs markedly from
that published, and may pre-date it.
Zweig MS 74, f.1. Autograph. 265 × 348 mm.

75 Paul Hindemith (1895–1963): *Trauermusik* for viola and strings,
1936
Writing to Sir Adrian Boult, Hindemith described this work as 'our
Music of mourning which I wrote in one of the BBC's dungeons in
January 1936 the day after his Majesty died . . .'. This is the short
score he wrote out then (the solist enters in the fourth system down),
and annotated when he gave it to Sir Adrian in 1961.
Add. MS 60500, f.2. Autograph. 318 × 240 mm.

To Michael Mullman

Symphony in E minor I Allegro

76 Ralph Vaughan Williams (1872–1958): Symphony in E minor, 1944–47
The opening bars of the full score. This is the sixth of Vaughan Williams's symphonies, though it was not originally published with a number. At first the symphonies were either given names ('A Sea Symphony', 'A London Symphony', 'A Pastoral Symphony') or were simply known by their keys. He returned to this key of E minor for his last symphony, the ninth.
Add. MS 58072, f.1. *Autograph.* 375 × 250 mm.

77 Benjamin Britten (1913–1976): Serenade for tenor, horn and strings, op. 31, 1943
The composition sketch of the setting of John Keats's sonnet 'O soft embalmer of the still midnight', the last number in the cycle before the epilogue for solo horn. Elsewhere the vocal line is simply marked 'tenor'; here Britten uses the initials of Peter Pears, the artist he had in mind and who gave the first performance at the Wigmore Hall in London on 15 October 1943.
Add. MS 60599, f.14. *Autograph.* 362 × 270 mm.

Suggestions for further reading

The New Grove Dictionary of Music and Musicians (1984) is indispensable to anyone wishing to investigate further after reading this book. It gives general information under many headings, and its bibliographies provide a guide to further reading on individual topics and composers. In addition, the long article 'Sources' gives editions and other bibliography for the more important early manuscripts.

The following British Library publications are concerned with specific aspects of the collections of music manuscripts.

P. J. WILLETTS The Henry Lawes Manuscript (1969)

P. J. WILLETTS Beethoven and England (1972)

A. HYATT KING A Mozart Legacy (1984)

The Library has also published complete facsimiles of some of the best-known manuscripts:

Ludwig van Beethoven, Autograph Miscellany from circa 1786 to 1799. (The 'Kafka Sketchbook') (1970). Edited by J. Kerman.

Johann Sebastian Bach: Das Wohltemperirte Clavier II (1980). Introduction by D. Franklin and S. Daw.

Franz Schubert, Piano Sonata in G major, op. 78 (D. 849) (1980). Introduction by Howard Ferguson.

Ludwig van Beethoven, Sonata for violin and piano, op. 30, no.3 (1980). Introduction by Alan Tyson.

Wolfgang Amadeus Mozart, The Six 'Haydn' String Quartets. (1985). Introduction by Alan Tyson.

Wolfgang Amadeus Mozart, The Late Chamber Works for Strings. (1987). Introduction by Alan Tyson.

A general survey of the British Library's music manuscripts will be found in A. Hyatt King A Wealth of Music (1983), where there is also a list of articles written about individual manuscripts.

78 Sir Michael Tippett (born 1905): King Priam, 1962
This page from the ink full score (the last stage in Tippett's compositional process) shows the moment in Act II where Achilles appears before the walls of Troy uttering his fearful war cry, intent on avenging the death of Patroclus.
Egerton MS 3786, f.75. Autograph. 360 × 262 mm.